Unveiling the Mind

Beatriz Badikian-Gartler

Copyright © 2014 Beatriz Badikian-Gartler

All rights reserved. No part of this book may be reproduced in any manner without the express written consent of the Publisher, except in the case of brief excerpts in critical reviews or articles. All inquiries should be addressed to: Pandora Lobo Estepario Productions, 1239 N. Greenview Ave. Chicago, IL 60642

All rights reserved.

ISBN: 1940856078
ISBN-13: 978-1-940856-07-0

Library of Congress Control Number: 2014907604

DEDICATION

To Oliver, Adelaide, and Ezri

for they are the future

Contents

Betrayals of the Body 1
    Drowning 3
    Fainting 4
    Falling 5
    Raging 6
    Sinking 7
    Throbbing 8

Counting Backwards 9
    Counting Backwards 11
    Dancing with Sonia 12
    New Year's Eve 13
    Polio 14
    Running away on my birthday 15
    Stories I will never write 16
    The Playground 17
    The Poetry Workshop 19
    The small things in life 20

Pomegranate Seeds 21
    A monument 23
    I have been painting on leaves 24
    In the garden 25
    Memento mori 26
    Neither here nor there 27
    Our work 28
    Pomegranate seeds 29
    Smash and scatter 30

Terra Mater	31
This is for the woman	**33**
After our damp skins	35
Everyday Gestures	36
Packing for the future:	37
Ripe Mangoes in Quincy, Illinois	38
This is for the woman	39
Women Who Sleep On Stones	40
Union Pier	**41**
First Day	43
Discovering Nature	44
Living in the country	45
Memorial Day Picnic	46
Fog	47
Beach Day	48
From the city	50
Solitude	51
Rainy Day	52
Small towns	54
Last Day	55
Unveiling the Mind	**57**
Adelitas *	59
Bones	61
In the Sumpul River	63
The writing studio in Johnson, Vermont: September 2001	64
Caption under a newspaper photo:	66
Unveiling the mind	67

v

ACKNOWLEDGMENTS

ACKNOWLEDGMENT IS MADE TO THE FOLLOWING PUBLICATIONS IN WHICH SOME OF THESE POEMS ORIGINALLY APPEARED.

Cantología
Journal of Modern Poetry
Fifth Wednesday
After Hours
Blue Lake Review
River Poets Journal
Ink and Ashes
Moon Journal
Prairie Moon
Her Mark Datebook
Seeding the Snow
Entre el Corazón y la Tierra
Shards of Light

BETRAYALS OF THE BODY

Beatriz Badikian-Gartler

Drowning

They say asthma is the fear of losing your mother.

Unable to breathe -- at 5 or 6
or 8 -- I'd call on all the neighbors to surround me
and scare death away. At night
I'd sit up on my narrow bed and gasp
and choke, trying to suck some crumbs of oxygen out of
the sad air, to fill my crowded lungs, and stay alive one more
day. Drowning in this manner became routine,
one more desperate fact of life in that home,
where disease gave us a reason for living.

Fainting

There is a herd of goats in Kentucky
who freeze and faint, unpredictably. A sudden voice,
a wheel drumming on the gravel road
will stop them dead in their tracks. Just fall over
like a ripe plum off a tree. Some go down quickly
and together, others – clumsier – fall slowly. We
share the fifth chromosome, these goats and me,
the interference with glycine receptors says
the medical text book, *the body's darker fortunes*
proclaims the poet. Startled out of our wits, our minds,
some of us scream and sob, others
faint, a few jump out of windows, breaking their jaws.

Hyperekplexia has no cure, says the textbook, *it is
inherited. It runs in families, on the mother's side.*
We break, we rise, we do what we're here for.

Falling

Falling,
falling,
never landing quite gracefully. When I was young
(and even now)
I'd fall often,
trip first, fall later actually,
because of my bad leg,
my bad foot actually. Polio plucked a muscle out of
my right leg, the one from your knee to your big toe,
left the right foot with little control,
less power.
Unable to bend my ankle upward, the foot falls
downward – a head bent over disconsolate and glum,
the red hibiscus spent and dried. It catches on carpets
and rugs, on raised sidewalks, stumbles and falls,
one leg in front, good and strong, the other
behind, useless as an afterthought.

Raging

In Delvaux's "Phases of the Moon" the women
stroll absent-mindedly or
hold their heads with one hand,
a blood-red bow on their breasts. Two men
with black moustaches and glasses study
their protruding bellies, their black crotches.
A waning moon above the trees and
rooftops foretells their future, slim and bloody.
I'm weighted down by my amplitude, whispers the brunette
by the window and I know what she means.
Weighted down by fluids I rage, I
cannot sit quietly
nor stroll happily.
I am a thing
who cannot stand her own skin,
brown and tight,
who cannot speak without shouting,
my own voice
a seagull's desperate cry.
I am a woman
who rages towards nothing and nobody,
which is to say
towards everything and everybody.

Sinking

Sinking,
sinking,
I sink into the vertiginous black hole and disappear
from the mirror's returning gaze, swallowed up
in one
swift
gulp.
It always happens this way:
sudden and inevitable
like a plane crash, the phone ring,
the summer shower.
Where do these ghosts come from and
how do they find me?

Throbbing

The vein
that hammers blood and pumps
blue, pulsating.
The head
that misbehaves, that rebels and
goes her own way.
The knife
of light and sound, stabbing
behind the eyes.
The throbbing of blood inside the vein inside the head.
And I
crave silence,
darkness,
some kind of peace.

COUNTING BACKWARDS

Counting Backwards

When she can't fall asleep she
counts backwards from one hundred
ninety-nine ninety-eight ninety-
seven When her heart races and
pounds she counts backwards *ninety-*
six ninety-five When anxiety threatens
her with fainting she counts backwards *ninety-*
four ninety-three Sometimes the numbers
get lost in the shuffle of so many thoughts
creeping unwelcomed and she has to start
over again from *one hundred ninety-nine*
ninety-eight ninety-seven Counting backwards
is hard work. It requires concentration. It demands
fortitude and patience *ninety-six ninety-*
five ninety-four Counting backwards
serves many purposes *ninety-three ninety-two*
And it's portable *ninety-one ninety* She counts
while riding the bus to work in the morning, sitting
in the café at noon, walking home or simply
waiting *eighty-nine eighty-eight* Numbers
appear behind her eyes *eighty-seven* Fingers type them
up in air *eighty-six eighty-five* Heart slows
down. Lips draw a smile *eighty-four eighty-three*
eighty-two eighty-one eighty seventy-nine

Dancing with Sonia

"If I can't dance, I don't want to be part of your revolution."
Emma Goldman

We dance among the broken steps,
the jagged edges of unfinished buildings.
Dance girl dance. Snap your fingers,
snap them above your head. Dance to live.
Live to dance. The ruins in Ancient Olympia
call you. People often asked us if
we were sisters. Last time we talked she said
as long as I can dance I'll be fine.
For forty years we shared dresses and
earrings, joys and sorrows, friends,
the quotidian and the extraordinary. We were
red diaper babies. My only solace now
is to write about her, about us. And in this way,
she remains in my heart and in my memories:
laughing, eating, dancing. In this way,
the unbearable sorrow her absence has brought
may fly away like the twelve white doves
that soared up to the sky above her resting place.

New Year's Eve
>(with thanks to Toni Morrison
>and Zora Neale Hurston)

He is my Ajax who brings me
a blood orange   red   red
dark red and sweet   I see
my first shooting star a few
minutes before the year ends
a new one begins   I make
a wish keep it secret   The sky
is black in Door County   the road
empty   We ride silently while tall
pine trees whizz by festooned with
Christmas lights shining in the dark
beacons guiding us towards our new
life   *too good to be true*   he says

He is my Tea Cake who teaches me
about music and painting   takes me
to the seashore and the mountaintop
yes, it's too good to be true   I nod
peeling my blood orange   Butterflies
escape filling every room in my heart

Incredulous at this new found love we
are like children swinging joyously
at a piñata that breaks open   Sweet candy
falling everywhere   We catch one piece two
blindfolded   trusting laughter all around us

Polio

On the hospital bed I sit,
my four-year old hands folded
on my lap. I wait. We all wait
alone in our pain: four, five,
eight year olds – my gaze glued
to the door of the vast children's
ward – tall beige walls, dark grey
tiled floors, windows fogged with
years of dust and grime, and sorrow.

On the white sheets I sit,
in the *Hospital de Niños*, frail
and dark. I wait for my mother,
for my father. We all wait.
A nun washes my face, combs
my hair. Makes me pray. *No
breakfast for you today* she says
and moves on to the black-haired
girl next to me, still asleep.

But, before mom and dad arrive,
two burly orderlies wheel me
down the hallway. *Where are
we going?* I ask in my small, brave voice.

In the O.R. the nurse
covers my face with a mask.
What is this? I ask again.
I don't hear the answer.

Running away on my birthday

I ran away last night:
I got in my car and drove
without stopping
going west on 55. Pressed that gas pedal all the way
down to the floor and never let off!
Drove
and drove until I had to pee or
eat.

I left everything behind
without even a note,
a phone call.
I drove for days on end, spent nights
in highway motels, eating
in small town diners,
taking my coffee to go. I drove
until my mind was clear,
white.

When I woke up I realized:
I don't know how to drive.
How does one run away then?
Hop on freight trains?
Walk and walk?
Take the Greyhound from one town
to another? From one town to another all
the way to the West coast?

Although —
I must admit —
nothing works for running away
like driving your own car.

Stories I will never write

I will never write about driving
a car or giving birth. I will never
write about how it feels to swim
in the deep blue sea. I will never
write about riding horses or
bicycles even though I tried both,
once. I will never write about
hoarding. I am a purger, a discarder.
I clean up, toss out, put away. I will
never write about being a sister or
an aunt. Being an only child has always
been my burden. I will never write
about not writing because I do, I
write, I am a writer who writes even
when I'm not writing. Because it settles me.
Because I have stories to tell.
Because,
when I read my writing,
I look at the audience and see their eyes.

The Playground

"don't like anybody" he says
refusing to play with the other kids
standing next to me
piling the rocks and sticks
one by one
adding a seed or two

"don't like anybody" he repeats
when the girl in the green frilly dress
touches his rocks and sticks and seeds
then he shrieks, he pushes,
he cries
I hold him I tell him to be nice

"don't like people" he shouts
when the boy in the blue pants and white shirt
takes his front loader truck away
I hold him I ask him to share
"don't like anybody" he reminds me
I should've known better

He knows what he likes and
what he doesn't: rocks, dandelions,
seeds, pasta, trucks, figs, these he likes.
Baths in the tub with rubber frogs and
yellow ducks, these he likes.
Taking a nap he doesn't.
Wearing socks he doesn't.
He likes blueberries and cherries,
goldfish crackers, lollipops.
He likes dreidles, sponges.
Stickers he adores.

He knows what he likes and
what he doesn't. He likes his nookies

and his blanky. He needs them to sleep.
His blue eyes, long eyelashes, dark
blond hair I like.
His cheeks red, his toes and fingers
I like.
I don't like it when he says:
"don't love nana anymore".

The Poetry Workshop

The white rectangular candle's flame in the center of the table flickers.
Two black bowls - one at either end – with red cherries glisten and
reflect the light above: the dark red and promising sweet fruits.
The white napkins hold the cherry pits and the stems too.
The sheets and sheets of white paper scattered
- the 8-1/2x11 kind - clutch poems, notes, story excerpts.
The pens of all types and colors - green, orange, black, blue – and
the pair of glasses and the red glass case and the red cell phone;
the water bottle and the plastic cup; one small blue book
and one small blue notebook; the neon green clipboard
and the black notebook. The rectangular table and
the chairs around the table; the women on the chairs;
the poems in the women; the poems on the table;
the poems in the books and in the notebooks and in the air
hovering,
hovering,
waiting to land.

The small things in life

purple and yellow pansies grow in the patio
brown ivy climbs the red brick walls
hopeful for green leaves and stems

sit out there
and read and
breathe

glimpses of sun shine among
the tall buildings and slanted roofs
bare trees waiting for Spring

the sky grey/blue
the wind took everything away yesterday
a dried-up gourd rolls around

a pair of doves comes to visit

POMEGRANATE SEEDS

A monument

Fifty-eight thousand twenty-two names
shimmer on a woman's white blouse.
Inside the black granite his black face fades.
A bird's red wings cut across his gaze like
brushstrokes on a canvas: the sky, a plane.

I have been painting on leaves

I have been painting on leaves.
Between waxed sheets of paper they sleep
when I'm not working on them.
Like looking at the gorillas in the zoo
behind their glass cage. Like the "boli"
in the Art Institute: mud, stick, blood,
and bone. "The pot is the thing that
bridges, joins together" says Heidegger, and
I begin to make vessels. Clay enters through
hand and eye, I enter the clay: we breathe in,
take a drink from each other. Body and
clay remember, touch, measure, and
record. Wisdom of the body.

In the garden

Kissing your hand in
the garden, the geraniums look
old, the pansies ragged, the petunias
droopy. Water has been absent for
a long time. Your eyes shine open
wide,
then look down
to your hand and my lips. The marigolds
smile conspiratorially.

Memento mori

I too will
one day
miss the scrumptious
cinnamon coffeecake of
the afternoons at 4. I too will
one day go away from this house,
this planet. Will the red
hibiscus on my window sill
remember me, the pink
cyclamen, the white jasmine?
Will the tiny enameled boxes
stacked up high in
the parlor think of me fondly?
Will the lonely blue umbrella in
the hallway?   At least
my poems
will bear witness
to my presence on this earth.

Neither here nor there

Neither here nor there I stand, one foot
on this side of the border, one on the other. Were
I to have three more feet, I'd easily place them on
three more lands. Neither here nor there, where
am I? And people say: you are everywhere, multiple,
you are fortunate. I respond: 'many' carries
the danger of becoming 'none'. Invisible I stand.

Our work

Our work is so different! You paint
bottles and stools, garbage cans abstracted,
an explosion of black on yellow, blue on red,
fish, leaves, an American flag, the sun.
Me?
one crazy lizard: red-green-yellow with blue
in the background, one small eye on the top,
one big eye all the way down. Rectangles
dialogue with circles, squares interrupt diamonds,
lines crisscross up and down, undulating. I like
the bright primaries, the scary greens and ominous
purples. You prefer white surfaces, clean black
lines, an orange in gray, an insect I don't recognize.

I paint my history in red and black, fill in
the blanks with pain and mourning, a melancholy-blue
sky,
a single word.

Pomegranate seeds

I like the shadow
of your left palm
on the tabletop while
you eat
pomegranate seeds
with the other. I watch you
deposit them
one by one
on the purply
rough surface
of your tongue
and
disappear
between molars and canines.

Smash and scatter

The waters break against
the ledge,
against
the shore, run
sideways.
Smashing waves scatter
fish and mussels, algae, make
the ground slippery.
Once
I saw a woman riding a bicycle by the lakeshore slide and fall,
break her   ankle,
writhe in pain,
white,
fainting.

Terra Mater

We come here for the violets. Wild,
purple and yellow, growing at the base
of a hollow tree. I sit at the edge, half
my body in sunlight, half in shadow. I turn
my head side to side, bending up toward
the warmth of light, curling back into
the loamy darkness. The gnarly-rooted presence,
the cave of a tree, the underground.

THIS IS FOR THE WOMAN

After our damp skins

pulled away from each other,
I could not see you
clearly
nor could you see me, your eyes
clouded over,
yet
our breaths – broken and shallow –

After our damp skins pulled away from each other,
the air between us filled
with electricity and moisture,
becoming something solid, thick and
dense,
yet
our breaths – fitful and brief –

After our damp skins pulled away from each other,
you stared at the empty space
in between before pronouncing my name
while my body shook,
cold and convulsive,
    yet
    our breaths --

Everyday Gestures
(after a photograph)

Each day begins alike.
A mother at the ironing-board, a father
at the assembly line. Both bent over. She

with the old coal iron
in one hand, the other
straightening out the cloth, a lock

of hair drawing a question mark
on her forehead. Wrinkles smoothed out
on a blue and yellow flowered dress. Are there

screaming children on the other side
of the door from where light
barely filters in?

His work,
the drudgery of everyday, and
the return home, spent yet empty.

Packing for the future:
               (after Lorna Crozier)

Take a pair of socks. Thick, blue or brown,
wherever you go, you'll have to walk. A velvet
pouch to hold the words, the seeds. White
underwear. Pounds and pounds of laughter
wrapped tightly in a rice paper sack. A few
gold coins, a water bottle. Just stuff
one bundle and put a stick through it, carry it
on your shoulder. Leave town walking
backwards to wave goodbye to the trees
and the neighbors. Packing for the future
requires discipline: know what you'll need
and take what you want. Take a pair of socks,
thick and brown, leave the rest behind. Paper?
Pencils? Who needs them! Speak your stories
to anyone who'll listen. Ask them
for a chicken leg in return, a slice of raisin bread.

Ripe Mangoes in Quincy, Illinois

In a Quincy hotel room, sitting on a green armchair by
the window I write and look out
at the grey-grey sky, feel the cold wind shaking
the small bush on the other side of the glass.
Is it me or the weather – turning everything
grey? Yet the whiff of ripe mangoes floating on by
cheers me up. They are on the desk, out there for all
to smell and eat. I wait for David to make the first gesture
towards peeling and cutting. They are so juicy! Hands get
sticky, juice runs down to the wrists, drips on everything
below, beneath. Perfumed flesh, yellow and
fibrous. Sweet to the point of disgust or
disillusion. Mangoes soft, ripe, ready to eat, on
the hotel room's desk in Quincy where I sit by
the window writing while my husband naps,
exhausted from driving all day. A grey sky
outside. The daylight wanes. More grey sky.

This is for the woman

This is for the woman who will not read this.
This is for the woman who is trapped inside a frame.
This is for the woman who cannot escape his words,
who cannot stop hearing her earlier voices,
who wants to be free of strings and fly,
who wants to write about others.
For the woman who hunches over fields of rice.
For the woman who escapes in the middle of the night.
For the woman who must write and requires readers.
For the woman who cannot stop the flow of time.

For all the women who need a place under the stars,
a room of their own, peace and bread.
For the women who taught me to struggle
and
for the women who listened.

Women Who Sleep On Stones

            (after Lucia Perillo)

are brave and tender at the same time.
They spread their blankets primly and
place a fluffy pillow on one end. Women
who sleep on stones ignite every night, their dreams
becoming a premonition: brick houses in cornfields,
weather-worn, solid, and dusty? Their hips creak now.
They can't rest on their backs.
They can't sleep on their bellies, their breasts
ache, squealing like bloated baby pigs. Women
who sleep on stones watch the stars move,
the sun rise, the spider's web shine. Next morning
they are exhausted, yet glad for their pain: stubborn
women who sleep on stones.

UNION PIER

First Day

The season of snow has given way to this month of May
when wildflowers tumble out of the darkness, strutting
their warm purples and deep yellows out on the prairie.
After this morning's rain, the sun slices in-between
impossibly-high red oak branches, its lukewarm rays diving
all the way down into the forest floor where
the smell of the wet woods rises
to meet my deep breathing.

Excited --
like children on Christmas morning -- we
descend the rickety, narrow steps to wander
on the wide beach, our bare feet sinking into
the unwalked sand, freshly dried and loose
between our toes. This is all ours! All ours
to contemplate and listen to and smell,
a peaceful pleasure for two, a miracle.
David skips stones into the lake's shining sheets
but I can't. I
don't know how
no matter how hard I try to hold the flat
pebbles just so, fling them straight out
with a twist
of the wrist, wishing for at least one bounce
or two. Before long, the fog -- that portent of cooling
temperatures -- begins to travel slowly overhead. With the mist
on our shoulders, our backs, we quicken our pace,
craving some warmth in the face of so much dampness.

And climbing the shaky stairs up to our newly rented cottage I
wonder how much of an urban dweller I am,
needing cellular phones and emails
to feel a part of this world,
when
a glimpse at a red cardinal perched on the slanted roof,
its black throat gleaming as he takes flight
should be enough,
when
in the black and quiet night the sound of waves crashing on the shore
should suffice.

Discovering Nature

How is a wave born —
water curling on itself
and folding over, a white-trimmed
edge of foam that leaves a trace
on the sand as it rushes back
to the lake? I can spend hours
watching the water come
to greet me, my naked feet wet
and sandy while the gulls hover
and dip suddenly, fly away
with their catch. And I
discover nature in my old age, able to
stop for a while and
watch and listen, silent
and still, the subtle splendor
of a cedar waxwing, the strident
beauty of the red cardinal
perched on an oak branch.

Living in the country

You're so lucky to live here
a lady exclaims while I
rock back and forth in
the faded green rocking chair on
the front porch, looking
out to the lake. *I wish
I did*, I tell her and
ponder: could I live here
all year round or would
the novelty wear off? Would
the bird watching
of every morning become
routine, abandoned after
a few weeks? Would
the lake become trite, one
more view
from the window? Would
the sound of the waves
become white noise,
unheard, ignored?

Memorial Day Picnic

We stop at a small cemetery and
spread our tie-dye, pink and
white blanket, gobble up cheese and
sausage sandwiches, hungry after
the long drive. In the distance,
beating drums herald the parade
marching down Main Street, far enough
away to be charming. I turn my head
up to the sun, finally warm enough
to face, after a long winter.

I am born again.

I open my eyes and – what do I see?
Suddenly
an indigo bunting lands
beside me to share our crumbs, his royal
blue feathers glistening, such a joy
to behold! What else can I ask for?

In the ravine beyond
and below, tree limbs
have fallen over
each other, a maze
of oaks, spruces, willows
and cedars. Birds
love these dead trees, their trunks full
of insects to eat and holes
to lay eggs in, to live
and die.

Fog

Fog today,
fog everywhere,
inside and out
where is the lake?
Fog enters through the half-
opened window, creeps
up the walls, rolls on the linoleum
floor, a fish leaps, somersaults, crashes
against the kitchen counter, blends with
the wooden staircase, and all become
one big ball of mist.
Will I get lost in my own house?
 A shell rolls in. If
I press it against my ear, I can hear
the voice of my own blood rising
high
above the dull chant of the stories
others have raised around me.

Beach Day

A calm lake Michigan
laps up its sweet waters on
the shore. The sky clearly
blue and clean of clouds, I
surrender my body to the stunning
sun. Stretching down on the sand I
spill down one shoulder at a time
along with each pelvic bone, first
the left side, then
the right. I mold a hollow where
my back finds its place,
carefully,
vigilant of sharp
pebbles, seashells, chunks of
green or brown glass, cigarette butts. I
breathe deeply two
or three times to
unknot each nerve, loosen
tendons and muscles. Though shut,
my eyes know the sun's
rays, their glow too robust for
my sheer eyelids, their heat penetrating
crevices and pores like
the slender threads of the surgeon, able
to patch together fragile membranes
with three or four swift stitches. All
peacefully warm now, the loud
squawks of the gulls above
startle me out of my slumber. I open
my eyes to see them delineating circles
and zigzags against the liquid sky,
screeching,
diving,
catching a fish.

Time to sit up and eat!

With one hand, I hold a ham and cheese
on whole wheat, with the other, shoo away
invisible flies. Not a bother really, perhaps
a small nuisance. What are minute insects
compared to this luxury, to these dazzling dreams I
inhabit daily, awake and certain.
Hours later, the rain storm comes.   Bright
filaments of lightning
illuminate the darkening sky and
the downpour surprises me on
my way back home. Furious
and sudden, the rain falls
on the hot asphalt,
raising steam, the woods becoming
the foggy background of a horror movie. This cooling
rain, welcomed and short, as
it should always be.

From the city

Today
friends from the city
come to visit. Proudly we
show them our beach, our birds,
the trees flanking the house, a canopy
of oaks and elms, pines and lilac bushes
in the backyard, the wildflowers in
the front. We name each one: white
trillium, false solomon's seal, dame's
rocket. They are impressed.

Later, I chop onions, slice tomatoes, wash
green lettuce, shave carrots, their orange
shards gleaming in the royal blue
salad bowl. The grill spews smoke
and the smell of barbecued chicken
fills our nostrils, waters our mouths. We
gather around the faded wooden picnic
table, sip cold beer, tell jokes, speak stories of
joy, of fear, of a shared past and a propitious
future, our lives held together somewhere
between our throats and our bones by
an invisible wire, pulling our breath, our words.

Hours later, the clouds, squeezing out
light, turn pink and blue, turn dark. When
the sun has finally dipped into the lake,
our friends return,
we stay.

Solitude

This morning's task: to identify the trees
in the neighborhood. Plucking a leaf
or picking up one off the ground I
observe closely its shape
  ovate or oblong
     its margins
  toothed or smooth
two or three lobed. I gaze at the leaf and
skim the guide to find its match – back and
forth, back and forth:
is it a red mulberry or an American sycamore,
     a northern red oak or an American elm?
Wandering the dirt paths in search
of natural knowledge can be a solitary
enterprise, unless you count the squirrels
and crows, the occasional possum, all
the birds. I find this solitude addictive,
dangerously appealing, tempting me
to avoid human contact. I force myself
to fight the seducer and find my way
to the intersection of Townline Road
and Red Arrow Highway, the only corner
in town that bristles with action:
the Country Kitchen, the Pumpernickel
Inn, LaDuke's Ice Cream and Confections,
the grocery store, the bakery, the auto
repair shop. The sun shines
hot and bright this morning. It's gonna
be a scorcher, the round lady in
the coffee-shop exclaims as I walk
in. And I am grateful for her words.

Rainy Day

All morning the wind
shudders the windows, pushes
a curtain of water against
the glass. Outside
each creature cowers
in its shelter. Inside I
listen to the furious
lake and the death-cries
of the wind while words
advance
   one by one
      across the lined pages of
my notebook, its blue covers
thick and velvet-soft. There is
something desirable
about rain and
the solitude it brings. The possibility
of hours of un-
interrupted reading; an entire day
devoted to shaping a poem, carving each word
out of the void or simply plucking one
out of the hundreds lined-up at attention
like good little tin soldiers in my brain.

Later,
the sky
spent of its passion, serene
after thunder, I walk
into town, a book under my arm,
wet grasses brushing
against my bare legs, crisp air
and vivid blue sky
welcoming
all the creatures out
again --
a red-headed woodpecker
who dives noisily against

the dead high limbs
of a sycamore tree,
its curling bark exposing
the whitish-brown trunk;
a cedar waxwing, his cinnamon
crest darting
in and out
          of a drenched thicket
of red mulberry leaves, quick
bursts to snack on flying
insects. I
prefer a cup of coffee, a slice
of peach tart at the Pumpernickel Inn.

Small towns

A squad of redwing blackbirds
perched on wire fences squabbles
their short, harsh syllables. Swallows
overhead chase insects. Driving
through the back roads of small towns we
catch glimpses of abandoned gas
stations, rusting road restaurants, a self-
service vegetable stand:
Take your strawberries and leave the money in the basket.
We trust you.

In South Haven, the soda fountain still
stands in the old department store dispensing
hot fudge sundaes and banana splits in clear
thick glass dishes, the aluminum stools covered
in red vinyl still spinning and swiveling, our legs
dangling way above the linoleum floor. Life
is mostly slow here, mostly
good, but then --
life is always better
when you're on vacation. To the small harbor
we saunter after our sweet break. A green
heron stands near the shore, unmoving, mulling
like a question, well-camouflaged among
the deeply green weeds that stand up straight,
the cattails splitting their seams, grey shadows
drawing their cover over sailboats, the water,
the pier. On the drive back I glimpse a llama
sitting in a field. She's far away
from her real home, I muse, and feel sorry for her.

Last Day

Blue jays on the porch!
Hurrah!
Hurrah!
A bright red cardinal lands
on the roof of the house
next door and sits there
in all his glory,
fiery and masked.
Finches flit
in and out of scrub brush,
all one witness of this holiness,
this natural world
we're giving up soon. Later, when
the stars fill the sky like distant
lights we'll take our last walk
on the beach. We'll notice the moon
once again
sailing out above the black lake, above
the earth, among the constellations:
Orion, Cassiopeia, Centaur, yet,
unlike a whole priesthood of sky watchers
before us, we will not know
what we're gazing at in that raw hole
shimmering, studded. We'll only grasp
the fortune of our short lived expedition
and lament our imminent loss.

UNVEILING THE MIND

Adelitas *
    After a photograph by Agustin Casasola

[Sing]
Si Adelita quisiera ser mi esposa, si Adelita fuera mi mujer,
le compraria un vestido de seda para llevarla a bailar al cuartel.

You stand on the train's wooden steps, your big
black eyes dart left
first, then
right,
left,
then right, calloused hands holding firmly onto the handlebars
lest your feet become entangled in the ruffles of your long
white skirt, the yellow rebozo flying behind you
where the other soldaderas sit
    or stand
among straw baskets filled with tortillas and a few
tomatoes, *aguacates*, corn, rice, coffee and sugar.
And today's laundry, bleached white under the Mexican sun. Waiting
to hear the whistle and see the smoke of departure,
what
do you see Angela? Is
the enemy nearby or
are you safe for now? Where is your compañero this morning?
sleeping inside the train, resting from a long
trek in the mountains the day before - or -
fighting as we speak, for a just tomorrow?

***

I don't need a man's organs to be a soldier, Angela Jimenez told the general
who protested her presence in the army. And
I wouldn't hesitate to blow out the enemy's brains
if I have to. Wrapped in her purple *sarape*, rifle in one arm and
baby in the other, she offered the infant her breast. And later,
carried the wood and the water into the village, the women
always the first to enter a town, to tend the fire and feed the men
who followed. Nights always found her on the field cot, unfolded

and
ready.

***

Tomorrow the soldiers will round them up, four
or five
or six
in a tight circle of rope, their flesh bulging, standing among the dry logs
of the fast burning fire that will ignite their muslin petticoats first,
their hair next, the smell of burnt flesh flooding the fields and
the mountains, carried in the wind as a secret message.
They will not cry nor plead. As the last tongues of flame leap upward,
they will yell
hijos de puta, you will die like the sons of whores that you are,
broken skulls and
bullet-ridden breasts piled high
in one scorched heap.

"Adelitas" was the name given to the women who accompanied the male soldiers during the Mexican Revolution of 1910. They served as companions as well as helpers, cooking, cleaning, and serving as look-outs for the army. They were also called "soldaderas."

Bones

> To the people of Central America who resisted and fought and died.
> And especially the women.

Bones are our last and best witness explains the forensic
pathologist, uncovering one hundred and eighty children's
bodies under the floor of one shack in *El Mozote*, their clothes
still hanging on their frail skeletons, red toy trains and
pink plastic dolls still hiding in their pockets. They lie

one
on top
of another

each one's head pierced by a bullet from behind. The flesh
gone, the bones remain, tortured and painfully
dead. *When I die*, the doctor requests, *use my organs, put the rest
in a simple coffin. I want to be a skeleton
as soon as possible.* The children of El Salvador had no choice of coffins nor
of what to do with their hearts and hands, their livers and eyes.

***

Rufina Reyes knows death intimately. It penetrates her one afternoon
through her pupils and her mouth, through the soles of her feet
as she kneels by a tree,
not moving,
not speaking, just listening
and watching.
Rufina squats in the shade, silently terrified as the hours pass: one,
two, three, four, counting every minute by the sound of
gunshots, heard clearly through the palms of her hands covering
her ears. Counting the hours by the screams of her children: *mama,
mama Rufina, help us.*

***

Eighteen years later,
when Rufina sinks her shoes in the reddish mud of the village and
lifts cotton shirts and faded dresses, worn thin
under the earth, a toy truck
falls out of her son's pocket.   *Hijos de puta*!
is all she can say, sons of
whores exclaims this old-fashioned young woman, swearing
on the lives of the soldiers, and asks:
why was I spared? why am I the only one alive? And answers:
To tell the story, that's why.

Rufina doesn't cry anymore.   No one does in *El Mozote*.   Crying

is a mere bodily function.

And the dead

demand

memory.

In the Sumpul River

Fleeing from soldiers, the woman
waits
for death
trapped
      between two rocks in the Sumpul river and
watches the buzzards flying low, *zopilotes anunciando la muerte.*

Will her bones bear witness to her presence on this earth?
Will the river scatter them against the sandy shores
or deposit them in the anonymous blue ocean,
a treasure,
a talisman?

The writing studio in Johnson, Vermont: September 2001

First week
Monday morning:
On the plane your left knee gives way, collapses.
Why don't you ever remember
to get an aisle seat?
Not to carry heavy bags?
To stay home?

Tuesday morning:
You sit on the porch, your left leg
up on a chair, ice on your knee: chickadees,
blue jays, goldfinches, hummingbirds,
wrens. The Gihon River runs
next to you. The bridge crosses it. Clouds
cover the sky. Everything you need
is within walking distance: cafe, restaurant,
the post office, a bookstore, the Red Mill building
where you dine. The house next door has a mouse.

Wednesday morning:
You sit in your studio
feeling better every day. Yesterday it poured
and stormed.

Wednesday afternoon:
You meditate: *sit like a rock*
the teacher says - strength and stability : Buddhism,
vicissitudes. The space
more important. Fear is good:
develops bravery,
eyes open.
Your knee still stiff, a little weak.

Second week
Monday afternoon:
A breeze blows while the sun

shines warmly. A gathering in
the meadow, wine, reading aloud, talking.

Tuesday morning:
What can you say?
Your hands shake.
You cannot eat.
You are afraid.

Tuesday afternoon:
In the dining hall
spirit talk.
all silent.
Jane bangs on a bowl.
Energy to those who are here. To those who are there.

Yesterday was sunny and warm. You sauntered
to the swimming hole in search of birds to watch.
Today is sunny and warm. You heard the news on the radio.

Yesterday you watched the tarot cards predict your future.
Today you watch the television screen, the horror,
frightened at what they tell.

Such chaos!
Dust and rubble too.
Twisted steel and concrete in shambles.
"Everything is connected, everything changes,
pay attention" says the poet. Pay attention!

Caption under a newspaper photo:
(a found poem)

"Search continues. A resident
tugs on a bag of belongings
scooped up by a backhoe Thursday
during the ongoing retrieval operation
at the Payatas
garbage
dump
in Quezon City, Philippines. At least
216 people died
after a wall of rubbish collapsed
on a squatter community
last week. More than 100
are still missing. President
Joseph Estrada said
he will not reopen the garbage dump."

Unveiling the mind

for Nawal el-Sadawi

Although your brother
failed in school, he was rewarded
by playing outside. You,
who succeeded,
were rewarded by working in the kitchen.
The schoolbooks said:
the stars were created by God.   But –
who created God? you asked.

An explosion of white hair,
every life is important , you say.
Write your life.

In prison, paper and pen
are more dangerous
than guns. You wrote your memoirs
on smuggled out toilet paper with
an eyebrow pencil
from a prostitute; you hid them
in a tin can under the floor. The guard
never found them. Writing more
necessary than breathing, you ask:

Why do we write?
And answer: *Not to die, to be immortal.*
And demand the unveiling of the mind.

PUBLISHER
Pandora lobo estepario Productions Press
http://www.loboestepario.com/press

Cover Art Work:
Beatriz Badikian-Gartler

www.ingramcontent.com/pod-product-compliance
Lightning Source LLC
Chambersburg PA
CBHW031212090426
42736CB00009B/889